seamless

MONOGRAPH PUBLISHING

Library of Congress Cataloguing-in-Publication data

Wright, Ralph OSB
seamless

Design by Ellie Jones
Cover Design by William E. Mathis and Ellie Jones
Cover Photo by William E. Mathis
MathisJones Communications, LLC

Published by Monograph Publishing, LLC
1 Putt Lane
Eureka, Missouri 63025
636-938-1100

ISBN# 978-0-9850542-2-9

seamless

Ralph Wright, OSB

PROLOGUE

"It is the honourable characteristic of Poetry that its materials are to be found in every subject which can interest the human mind" - so read the opening lines of the 'Advertisement' or Prologue to the Lyrical Ballads of Coleridge and Wordsworth published in 1798. After describing the poems that the book contains as 'experimental' Wordsworth, writing anonymously, goes on to say: "It is desirable that readers should not suffer the solitary word 'Poetry,' a word of very disputed meaning, to stand in the way of their gratification; but that while they are perusing this book, they should ask themselves if it contains a natural delineation of human passions, human characters, and human incidents; and if the answer be favorable to the author's wishes, that they should consent to be pleased in spite of that most dreadful enemy of our pleasures, our own pre-established codes of decision."

These poems, too, are offered for the pleasure of the reader whoever he or she may be. They are the product of the past fifteen or twenty years of my life as a monk. It is considered more hazardous these days to put one's 'vision' into poetry: people immediately feel uneasy and talk of propaganda. But perhaps it is when we cease to try to share our deepest thoughts, feelings and beliefs – about God and love and sin and silence and violence and hatred and union and distance and time and eternity – that our poetry ceases to please or to inspire. I would like my poetry to be read and loved not only by poets but also by the non-poet clientele of our world. Men and women of every walk of life and every interest. From those who program computers or punch cash registers to those vice-presidents who make multi-million dollar deals and survey the world through the dark one-way windows of tall buildings. For we all have to cope on an almost daily basis with belief, unbelief, love, loyalty, betrayal, union, violence, pain, ecstasy, joy, depression, sickness, anger and death.

The poems that follow are attempts to capture moments from these common experiences and to hold them up boldly and without shame for others to share. The Christian sees the dark side – sin, tragedy, separation, death. But he also sees the awesome beauty of all that God creates and the extraordinary dignity of Man re-created in Christ and called to share eternally in the intimate life of God. He already experiences in part the peace of his risen Lord and he believes that it is possible here and now to know, in some measure, the deep joy of union with God. He wants his faith to be reflected in his life and in his words for his deepest call is to give to others from his store – of life, of hope, of vision – whatever has been entrusted to him. If these poems are instances of this, I hope they may succeed in communicating a little of this vision especially to those who, perhaps seeing almost nothing hopeful, may be on the verge of opting for despair.

CONTENTS

seamless

POEM

a poem is an acrid
semi-ecstatic
immaterial
sneeze
breaking beautifully
out of silence
after a moment's
pause
poised
outside history
taking flesh in scrawl and revealing
the mind's mystery

THROUGH A GLASS DARKLY

only a thin
film of glass
protects the moth
as it bangs
again and again
against the light
in the dark night
from the sizzle
of extinction

ALTHOUGH DUST

(John 17: 23)

Although dust
I am loved
by the one
eternal
Son of the Father
just as intensely
as this same Father
loves his one
eternal Son

O mystery
O majesty
O wonder
that what we
in our wildest dreams
could not conceive
has been
by God's own Word
quietly revealed

WOMAN

within her
and of her being
comes one to be
who will not cease

she speaks each day
God's Word made men
uttered again, again
and again
into our silence

hers is a dignity
that none may measure
hers a patience
refined by fire
hers a majesty
unperceived
in the painful tedium
of giving birth

the mystery
of her being
echoes the mystery
of God creating

and out of darkness
Light

MARY

the young girl gazes
at the dark still waters
of Siloe
her smile reflects the ecstasy
of her surprise —
surprise at her young self,
surprise at God,
at children, priests, camel-sellers,
camel-dung checkers, donkeys
and all the Temple turmoil
of being NOW and being alive —
she feels the calm of that full-shading love
that wraps her round
and in the shadow of this deep content
she knows what God's own power could do in her
at the appointed hour

GREAT CALM

I am filled with joy
that God loves you
with great competence
for my love is infinite
in clumsiness—
when I wound
He heals
when I damage
He restores
and you are always
in his hands
O great calm
O mighty God
O quiet joy

BECOMING MAN

The humble moment
of total fusion
in darkness
and silence
seen by no one
heard by no one
felt by no one
a greater detonation
than any nuclear fission
and for a long while yet
no one will know it has happened.

THEY TRACE MY BLOOD

they trace my blood
through generic Adam
back to the first
life on the planet
—a continuity that does,
I must confess,
boggle the mind—
but God made me
as if He had made
no other one
no other where
for a Lover
each person happens
NOW
and no other when

CONCEIVE

to bring
and to have brought
into being
through God

one called
to live forever
intimately
with God

what a stunning
mind-scalding
thing to do
and to have done

could anything
conceivably
be greater —

TRANSPLANT

The surgeon, master of the arts,
has learnt to plant organic parts
but never will and never can
effect a change of heart in Man
for God alone
has the craft
in place of human hearts of stone
to graft his own.

REFLECTIONS

The prism of the mind explodes the world
into a million colors
a dazzling university
with too little time for wonder

wonder at the way a leaf may fall
simply at evening into half-still waters
that till this moment held a silent face
peering
out at the dying day.

A MIND FOR WONDER
for T.S.E.

I

Preferring my blindness
to your vision
I must make
my way into
every cul de sac
bang my head on
every ceiling
fall into
every pit
poison my bloodstream
and brain
by imbibing
every kind of chemical
drink myself
into and out of
every delirium
make and lie in every kind of bed

because I no longer trust
the wisdom of your eyes
and of your tears
no longer wish
to learn
from the long generations
of your follies
but prefer
the excitement
of exploration
and the adventure of falling

into no matter what
dungeon of despair
to that of finding out
where
I am — and keep —
going

even the rats would weep.

II

It is the absence of vision that is crucial
(nobody is blamed for being blind
except perhaps Oedipus)
and vision is gift:
gift that reveals, unveils, unwinds
the wool from the eyes
to provide — so unexpectedly —
light at the end of the sewer.

It is the vision that leads us
into pocket size inner galaxies —
the livre-de-poche-size bible with all
the world of divinity
casually caged in our minds —
lock the Word
into your hearts, someone said,
knowing that this would spell freedom
freedom from the anarchy of blindness
freedom from being
lost
in a dense jungle
or a desert
with no indication in three hundred
and sixty degrees
of the right way to water.

Our blindness is brutal, congenital and,
unless it makes us aware
of the vision as gift,
lasting.

But in our blindness, hitting our heads
against each beam or ceiling and falling down
each flight of stairs,
the need for ignorance may dawn on us
starkly
so starkly that we blaze a way
beyond the brute computer
penciling out with awesome competence
its finite balance of a billion billion
facts, back to interstellar ignorance.

If, in this systematic gloom
with news upon the hour,
there can yet be
space for ignorance
God's word may be a rocket to our minds
launching us upon a vast journey
into an ignorance
greater than we could conceive.

As at the top of the tent
the trapeze artist
hangs and swings with jaws tight
in the mouthpiece held
in her partner's teeth
the audience stunned
watches with awe
the ultimate test of dependence,
so in our chosen darkness
the spirit waits
for the birth of the Word,

the touch and the taste
of God.

The water, the fire, the blood
telling
of three kinds of union
with the calf lips thrusting against
the ultimate udder

and the meaning that dawns
is
union without dissolution

the union that dawns between finite and infinite
is
wholeness without explosion

the dawning of permanent joy
is
ecstasy without mitigation

and in the vision given
gently as gift
to the gladly blind
with the empty hands
all becomes glory.

THE BIG MYTH IS THAT
THERE'S TOO LITTLE LIGHT

The big myth is that there's too little light
for us to see by — but there's far too much.
The shadows from small gravel in the dusk,
the magic and magnificence of seasons,
or leaves turning from green to gold to rust —
are all too full of the mind of the Creator,
they leave us blinded and absorbed by dust.

Dust is our medium and we mold it firm
to build a plastic heart and reach the moon.
Things have become idols and our minds
feed on distractions leaving little room
for silence or monogamy in prayer.
Someone has opened the camera to expose
our vision to the swift assault of light.
All of our wonder is being drowned by dust.
O not too little light but far too much.

PYROGENETICS

the widening mystery of exploding light
dazzles our mind
Queen Anne's lace grows in milliseconds
and dies at once in half a mile of sky
purple turquoise gold and dazzling red
flares carve glory in the night
then fall back into nothingness

God in miniature
brings pilot galaxies into random being
snuffing them out in falling golden rain
amid a million gasps of stunned delight

one sudden cloudburst
hangs a cage above us in the air
a 14 ct chandelier of fire
descending slowly over frail skulls

and yet in all this masterpiece
poured out across the canvas of the dark
looms stark our human brevity
behind the blind amazement of our pyromania
still peer through
the petty twinklings of the Big Time stars

AS YOU PASSED BY ME

as you passed by me
lying
with nothing beautiful about me
helpless
caught in my sin
like a beast in a trap
you looked at me —
dark water with the distant stars
of deep love reflected
in all the calm of tenderness —
you didn't even have a chance to speak
they needed you elsewhere too quickly
but in your wake you left me
quickened into knowing
by that glance
my dignity in being loved by you

FROM ALL ETERNITY

from all eternity
You made me
as if to be
your only spouse
in time
may I choose You
to be mine

THE BODY OF CHRIST

Man holds
within his hand
the one who holds
within his hand
the universe —
cup your hand in awe, O man,
and pray
that He who comes so humbly
unto you
as food
may make you worthy of himself
eternally
as God.

ANTIOCH

Ignatius longed
to be wheat
ground pure
by the teeth of beasts
to become the strong
bread of life
fed to his brothers
the Body of Christ.

Was he glad
to be scourged pure
when the tongues of men
lashed him raw,
when his grain was broken
his grape trod
and he was used
for the Body of God?

O HIDDEN GOD

God finds it such a business staying hidden
with ski-masks, plastic gloves and moving
around only when all are drunk
or simply   sleeping
he has to be so sure to leave no trace
though sometimes in his carelessness he leaves
a kind of jet-wake in a sunset sky
or something like the slime a slug expels
to help its passage on a blade of grass
but mostly people overlook these clues —

If he should quit this game of hide-and-seek
— as often in our ire we tell him to —
and let himself be caught red-handed
selecting this one sperm for this one egg
or breathing the odd galaxy into being
what space for fun and laughter could remain?
we'd all have ulcers or be dead for awe.

THE GODMAKER

within the tightened nutshell of my mind
where I pretend to godhead
I make God
after my own image
God Who Is
impervious to all
the adumbrations of my wild desires
beyond before bestriding
without thought
the cataracting galaxies of years
I make an idol and ignore
the image given
and refuse
to let God be the kind of god who gives
the elbow-room I need for being wild
the kind of god who chooses to know wounds
and emptiness in place of full delight
the kind of god some dare to think prefers
— after so many eons of instant being —
to make a batch of things that fail a while
and leave them space and time in which to heal

TRUNCATE

Redwood trees
have soared in silence
for thousands of years
along our shores
their age
their calm
their dignity
command respect

scions thrusting
from the roots of Jesse
across our land
towards eternity
are axed daily
without awe
out of being

WHEN GOD MADE YOU

When
God
made
you
there
was
silence
in
heaven
for
five
minutes.
Then
God
said:
"How come I never thought of that before?"

CHEERY THOUGHT ON A RAINY MORNING

if You didn't need to
but only made me
because You loved me
what an unbelievably
marvelous being
I must be
designed
by the One Lover
only to be
perfectly beloved

BIRTHDAY UTTERANCE

I have great joy
in knowing that you
have been
born
into the world
because
having been breathed
by God
into existence
you will never
be able
 — like a bubble —
to pop
suddenly
back into nothingness
welcome
to this one great
champagne
dancing
party of being
and be
always
alive and utterly
grateful to Him
who
simply freely spontaneously
needlessly and
eternally
utters

MEDITATION FOR GOOD FRIDAY

let us test him with cruelty and torture
and thus explore this gentleness of his
and put his endurance to the proof (Wisdom 2.19. JB)

We have explored the gentleness of God
with nails against the bitterness of wood;
our pride and our unlovingness have torn
the good man and have drained him of his blood

Have you not seen the sorrow he has borne,
the sadness that has scarred him with its goad:
our apathy, our selfishness, our crude
and wounding words, whose wounds he hardly showed?

His body might be crushed and whipped and torn,
his gentle love be finite on our wood;
our pride and malice wore a way for blood
as we explored the gentleness of God.

But nails are not the ultimate in pain
and bodies feel quite soon the final goad
of death that presses home its blows with crude
hands that lack the gentleness of God—

while words can open timeless raging wounds
by stamping on the love a person showed—
the ultimate in pain that was his load
was learning that they did not know his God.

Forgive them O forgive them O forgive
all who have felt the bruising of the goad,
forgive them Father, O forgive them, Lord,
they have not known the gentleness of God.

Forgive us and enlighten us and draw
all who have nailed these gentle hands to wood,
forgive us all — we know not what we do—
as we explore the gentleness of God.

JERICHO

The man who fell in with thieves
on his way to Jericho
may have been going there
— for all we know —
to murder his mother

he may have come
from robbing the Temple
or sleeping with his next-door-neighbor's wife
— we are not told —

the man who finds him
half-dead
clearly does not know

and God seems to be hammering home
blow by blow
the thought
that worthiness is irrelevant

all we need
is to recognize need

MOTHER AND CHILD

uncoarsened
by the calluses
of daily decadence

you feel
the full repertoire
of human wounding

and with eyes
innocent
of all confusion

you see
there can be
no relief

before the iron
has been driven
the nerves

have screamed to silence
and the thing
has been done

THEOPHANY

A fine dry
stalk structure
on which are poised
with total symmetry
tiny windblown
toy umbrellas
forming a perfect
Fabergé sphere—
a Czar's jewel
beyond fury
good for nothing
but reflecting glory—
Yellow Goatsbeard
a dead weed
ripe
for launching seed.

IT IS THE MULTIPLICATION

it is the multiplication
of the number one
by six million
that horrifies
in Holocaust

but if it had been done
to one
person once
God would still have died
horrified

WORLD

our world a luminous
bubble of blue
uttered by God
blown by a child
poised in the dark
proud serene
floating in calm
royal ease
until the sun
explodes it into
sudden nothing

WAR

War forgets that men have mothers,
   keeping faces without names.
To kill with calm we must remain
distant — being brothers.

Numbers may be bombed at will,
   erased from charts and left in tombs.
But sons are made of love in wombs
   and persons are too close to kill.

DISTANCE GIVES THE MEN OF WAR THEIR HOLD

Distance gives the men of war their hold,
　kept to keep me capable of hate.
I cannot love the men I do not know
　and, lest I love, they keep between us space.

They character your person with black paint,
　feeding me a myth with subtle skill.
They keep me from the knowledge of your face
　— that I may kill.

Idea-logians smile and wash their hands;
　they quietly state the final terms for peace.
If they would let me know you as a man
　it would suffice.

SKULLPLACE

Skullplace — the site for crucifixion
both yours and mine —
skullplace — the seat of consciousness,
here's where the nerves
scream loud their oaths of agony
swearing at God at humankind at iron
hopelessness while lying hard
hammered against the earth —
skullplace — the final honing place of man
boned into being by some casual sperm
that kissed an ovum and became a child
to laugh in the light-time briefly and to dance
until abandoned like some broken hull
alone on the final hillside of this skull.

FALL '84

There won't be any leaves to fall next year
so take a long last look at them with awe
drifting in the sunlight this October
and splashing farewell across the canvas
in gentle reds and yellows, golds and browns.

After all the fallout and the ashes
God's trying something new for '85
in monochromes of grey and white and black
with nothing quite so dangerous this time
as color and life — they won't be back.

SOME PLACES IN THE WORLD ARE MADE OF PEACE

some places in the world are made of peace
require silence
sudden oases of calm
within an evergrowing overpowering
waste of noise
man builds playpens for his private wars
and petty hatreds
he litters them across the quiet hills
he finds waters full of godlight
dark with marble deep with mystery
stirs them troubled with a nervous hand
alive with lust
then curses when they won't reflect
the waiting face of God who gives them
only for wonder to our raging hearts
only for beauty
to men who quickly tire of stillness

COMPARED TO YOUR LOVE

compared to your love
for me
every insult
is an honor
every curse
a blessing
every frown
a smile

I am so overwhelmed
by your choice of me
from before the universe
that nothing
can disturb
my serenity
and joy

every uproar
is like a storm
on a teaspoon
in the flat calm
of the wide Pacific

RELATIVITY

The hands that made
the universe
we nailed
down to his own
dead trees
thought freezes when we notice
that this dark event
though light-speed traveling
out from our planet
cannot yet have reached
most of the stars

THE TROUBLE IS

The trouble is we try to look too far
And so don't live the day before our feet.
The years stretch on impossible to bear
But for the next few hours I still could keep

Treading the wheel and hoping that the clouds
Might part and leave at least a hint of sun.
Living the moment gives me space for joy
And keeps tomorrow's problems till they come.

This is the way to live a life of hope
Distilled into the moments that are given.
Surrender all of care into those hands
That have already known how nails are driven.

UNCOMMUNICATION

Thee is a kind of
welding power in
wounding words
that spells
excruciation
not the
one stab once stab once
but a million varied
lightning pointed
jabs that stab
the ever newly opened nerves
to make
one roaring silent
raucous wound
of hypersensitivity
probed by brine again
and yet again or graveled
into by the always sand or scythed
on angry razor coral with the world
on every side one
infinite needle

II

To communicate is our passion and our despair. —
Golding

tongued with the deep
Atlantic boom of a
thundering bell

or ringing light
with the tiptoe feet of the

ballerina
blue-bell dancing
words that can wring
from mute dumb
brute
incomprehension
oneness of laughter or lyrical
union alive—
O how I bruise
with scarred and sensitive
words
fists on their
smooth enchanting
rock-white fearful façade
numbed soon to all but the feeling
of raw and naked
nerves hurt
burnt
torn through concern at my
impotent tongue that remains
poised
hung to divide
hung to achieve hostility—
Christ in place of my
rude incompetence
give me the voiceless
cry of a child
breaking at Bethlehem
into history
with the total silence
of God's simplicity

III

iron splinters barb the pain that are my words
caught in the naked palms of my compassion
splinters that plunge deep deep

as the writing salmon ploughs with passion
the fly deep in the angry flesh
soon to be served
(at the request of some select Salome)
ice-cool with mayonnaise upon a dish—
my pain to hear the writhing at my words
pain at my verbal impotence pain at the booming
clatter empty hollowness of sound
palling upon raw nerves — words
that are unmine
borrowed from a huge coinage that remains
burdened with the Absurd—
O the brute blasphemy of wielding tools
that blunder clumsiness and make each try
at transplant mutilation
for I
cannot be you
the mute flat stone of fact upon this beach
remains unwashed by tides however high
I long to be and yet cannot be you
long for long unity and deep-denied

oneness of ecstasy that lightning knew—
again the thunder silences and I
must be content to be and not be you
must be content to stroll and hear
over my shoulder kettle drums that roll
beating my message smoke-rings into blue
out wherever the jungle reaches
towards you

I LISTENED TO THE SOUND OF RAIN

I listened to the sound of rain
upon the leaves
approaching with the wind
— the rain and wind were still some woods away

I listened to the terror of the wind
upon the leaves in anger tearing them
untimely out of life and swirling them
at random in the dark upon the ground

I listened to the calm that came
from nowhere on the leaves
when suddenly the angry air was gone
I heard them welcome with relief
the newborn silence of the night
and watch in awe for dawn

BLESSED

Blessed are those who are empty
    for they are filled with God.
Blessed are those who are open
    for they welcome the Spirit.
Blessed are those who are silent
    for they receive God's Word.
Blessed are those who are lost
    for they are found by God.
Blessed are those who leap
    for they are in God's hands.
Blessed are those who are blind
    for they receive their sight.
Blessed are those who are weak
    for in God they are strong.
Blessed are those who believe
    for they are the light of the world.
Blessed are those who surrender
    for in God they find peace.

LEAFSCAPE

there is a silence in the patience of the leaves
waiting in stillness for the breath of Fall
all the silence of the desert wastes
when no one roamed the planet —
there is a waiting in their watching mood
a resignation to a job well done
they clung to branches yesterday as wind
wrestled with them to release their hold
then drifted to a gentler breeze today
that rippled on the amber and the gold
with all the sigh of loam

PERSONS

I know a man with silence in his eyes
the silence of the moon shining
through trees on dark water
when seeing him I suddenly
knew calm
the calm that comes to one who walks
over heavy bramble-covered land
a long journey
and reaches road
I met his eyes we smiled and he was gone
but persons are forever

ONLY THE MAPLE
for Andrew aged eight

If joy were not so vulnerable to words
I would describe the way you are and all
Down through the unknown centuries to come
Would marvel at God's masterhand in you.

If joy were not so vulnerable to words
I'd catch the limpid laughter that springs
Out from the young mountain that is you
cascading in the sunlight.

If joy were not so vulnerable to words
I'd write the full simplicity of you
Exploring with your eyes and with your fingers
God's toy creatures.

*

Only the maple blazing its silent news
Tells of you and keeps the joy unbruised.

WARSHOCK

—*on looking at a picture in the Pentagon*

wide eyes
stare
out of nobody
into nothing

shell burst
mind burst
blind

like surf
men break
endlessly
on this beach

rippling the sand

A WAVE

a wave
of thanksgiving
like tear gas
hits me:

God hides
so completely
so discreetly

my senses
geigercount
his glory
in the rose

faith reaches
beyond

where all the light
of all the galaxies
is but a candle

so discreetly
so completely

thank you

PEOPLE TELL ME

People tell me "Don't be afraid of God,
for God is Love."
O don't you see
I fear the very Lover
in my God!

I fear the Lover
hiding glory in the drab disguise
of humble people

I fear the Lover
barely daring to reveal
his gentle breeze of being
lest majesty beget
tremendous homage

I fear the one who loves me
and touches with such tenderness
this fragile thing of freedom that is "me"
lest it be shattered

and yet perhaps I have no fear of God
but of his being Love
and so of me

I fear the fact that he is Love and so
must leave me all the drama of decision
that love requires
                   as sure as light reveals
and darkness veils, I too must choose

the narrow way, the holocaust, the bleak

leap of abandonment into the barely known
and yet demanding deep —
I fear the fact that I am made to choose
and so may lose

O EXTRAVAGANT

O extravagant
patient God
taking billions
of years to cool
molten light
till life might ripen
into consciousness
competent for your godhead

O unknown
humble God
choosing to come
without glamour
among the dung
of steaming cattle
and so become
"the eldest of many brothers."

O meticulous
lowly God
choosing to go
without magnificence
nailed between
your brother thieves
proving with un-
ambiguous deed
how pure the God
who so conceives

HUMILITY

Humility
is
hard
even
for
God
as
the
iron
passes
the
median
nerve
into
the
wood

GLORY

I have felt
the crucifixion
of the Word
upon the sidewalk
after the heavy rain
and the sound
was like one screaming
"I am a man
and no worm!"
but in the darkness
my foot
ignored
his glory

BROWN LEAVES

brown leaves
against a grey sky
make drab the spirit
but sunlight turns
Calvary into Tabor
gold red and yellow

waiting on the wind's whim
or racing quietly down
chasing their shadows
they know the measure
of their own magnificence
and with a hint of Handel's
Watermusic
welcome the friendly loam

IF MY ONLY

if my only
expectation
from the world
in this life
is crucifixion
what an amazing
calm
comes upon me
in the face of daily
minor tragedies
yet this is all
that God in Christ
has guaranteed
to those who walk his ways

GOD

God
spoke
to Elijah
in a gentle breeze
but after a storm
leaves
at sundown
in total stillness
have their own eloquence

THE WAY IS HARD

the Way is hard
long winding narrow
—sometimes steep—
through woods valleys
mountains deserts
"a lifetime's march"
while the World whispers
to hungry hearts
"turn these stones to bread"

but the Word coming
from the mouth of God
says "if a child
ask his father
for a loaf of bread
will he give him a stone?
I tell you this
that my joy
may be in you:
I and the Father are one"

they take up stones
to silence him
but he passes
through their midst
later they come
and he stands still
to let the grain
be harvested

taken pounded
ground to powder
yeasted kneaded

baked and offered
as food sufficient
for a day's march
—the Way is hard—
come take and eat
that your joy too
may be complete

I KNOW A MAN WHO HAS A FEEL FOR LEAVES

I know a man who has a feel for leaves
and treats them kindly as one might a friend
he feels that if a human being was cloned
and multiplied like paperbacks or waves
they still would have a being of their own
and would when gone be left in separate graves

so why not have a reverence for each leaf
like this one from an oak tree on this path
reaching like a hand towards who knows
what dying ecstasy as the slow breeze
helps it find a resting place or home
in the recycling earth?

He feels that it is worth
a moment's silence and believes
that anyone who ever has seen war
or heard of famines, floods or on the news
has watched the havoc that an earthquake strewed
with men and mountains in its wake ignored
— or even watched a stadiumfull applaud —
will pause with wonder as he looks and breathes
and also have a little time for leaves.

AT ANY MOMENT

at any moment
when my heart seethes
or my guts burn
I may compare
my agony
to another time and pain
and find
that mine
is only
a cheap low-key Gethsemane
and a poor man's crucifixion

PSALM 101

Given the current minimum wage
God changes the heavens,
the Psalmist says,
like a man
trashing a pair of socks
as not worth the darning time
and buying new ones.

We by radio catching waves
from stars that died
before God became Jesus
know eons more
about our brevity
and so need
to hear the Light
in one word Abba
declare or dignity
to the unmended night.

TOMORROW

Compulsively I rush towards
the next event
convinced that I have no time now
to be alive to what I do.

Why am I so ashamed to be
gladly what I am
that I toss back like beer
the vintage moment of my present being?

If I find no joy
in all that is
but only what will be
then I see nothing good
and make my life one long release of wind

THE BIRDS

the birds
make all
worth while

singing us
out of our
drab tragedies

into
a new
world

of sunrise
springtime
grace
and movement

a ballet
of
exuberance

before the silence
of winter
leaves only

a few
crumbs
scattered

in the omnipotent

wide
snow

CURRENT MOTION

we go faster
from A to B
than ever before
we live longer
machine aided
with veins restored

we count precisely
the grains of sand
on the sea shore
and guess plausibly
who would die
in a nuclear war

but find time
less and less
for what matters more
Who are we?
Where are we going?
What's the score?

WHEN THE LAST RIVER

When the last river has let its waters
meet the sea,
when the last cloud has let its rain
touch the waves,
when the last breeze has brought coolness
to the face of man
and the last sun has bowed its head
behind the mountains,
I will reach down and raise you up,
says the Lord,
to be with me, your brother,
for ever.

MESSIAH

anoint the wounds
of my spirit
with the balm
of forgiveness
pour the oil
of your calm
on the waters
of my heart

take the squeal
of frustration
from the wheels
of my passion
that the power
of your tenderness
may smooth
the way I love

that the tedium
of giving
in the risk
of surrender
and the reaching
out naked
to a world
that must wound

may be kindled
fresh daily
to a blaze

of compassion
that the grain

may fall gladly
to burst in the ground
– and the harvest abound

HOW MUST IT BE FOR GOD

How must it be for God,
who hides beneath a Calvary of pain
the massive love he has for each of us,
to know with absolute precision
the mammoth nature of our unconcern,
the cold of our indifference?

Yet he is so afraid of drawing love
for less than kosher motives that he hides
and chooses that his Son should not be seen
except within the guise of one despised;
and that his gentle love should stay unknown
except by those whose almost foolish trust
leads them to tread the path that he once trod
and know, as one ignored and mocked by men,
the wonder of the love beyond the pain.

OUT OF A DEEP

out of a deep
respect for silence
a poet speaks
without violence

he speaks to be heard
below the noise
with a quiet voice
but without reserve

not with the agony
of a Laocoon
struggling with snakes
for articulation

but with playful
hands that feel
his words like clay
on a potter's wheel

he accepts the gentle
humiliation
of time and space
in anticipation

of the final moment
of eternal union
beyond music
beyond illusion

UNSURPRISED BY DARKNESS

if God's own Son
had to brink despair
dying in the darkness
of noonday night

why should I
know a tranquil passage
from finite groping
to infinite Light

why am I shocked
by the daily trauma
woven into
the heart of flesh

the rending anger
perdures from the womb
till the hands are folded
in the calm of death

see the stars
and ponder the Word
in whom each galaxy
finds its being

then watch the one
whose humble coming
respects the measure
of our seeing

for "who can live
with a blazing fire?"
O mercifully mercifully

hidden God

coming as breeze
coming as bread
coming through the grape
our feet have trod

GLIMPSES

Sometimes I write poetry
heavy with obscurity
mirroring the distance
between I "am" and "should."

Sometimes words flow from me
guileless in simplicity
capturing a moment's mood
of being what I could.

Why am I so tempted
when laden with complexity
to jettison these glimpse words
limpid, pure and good?

Simply because a long glance
in megawatts of sanity
would burn away the retina
of mind and heart and blood.

I HAVE SUDDENLY BECOME

`

I have suddenly become
happy with the passingness of things —
time no longer seems mainly
taking things away in leaps and bounds
but bringing ever more and new things to me —
I seem to ride an Amazon of water
moving to an ocean of fulfillment
and infinite reunion

SEAMLESS

Stretched between tall grass in the dawn light
the cobweb shimmers—
rainbows,
magic innocence,
routine evil.

The fighters with folded wings
stand at parade as the carrier moves
through Mediterranean blue,
inspected annually by the Queen
an admiral at each elbow.

Even the spider moves like a priest
towards his breakfast sacrifice,
but how does the fly feel
caught on the wire
before and after the jaws?

I sat at the back of the church.
Under the dome a spider hung
caught like a copter in the sun.
A tiny lump of gold it soared and plunged,
soared and plunged.
A trapeze artist high in the Big Top.
A secretary typing a routine letter
in total silence.
A seamstress mending a torn and seamless robe.

BIOGRAPHY OF RALPH WRIGHT, O.S.B.

Ralph Wright was born in Nottinghamshire, England, about 200 yards from Sherwood Forest on October 13, 1938. He was christened David Grant Melville Wright. His father, Monty Wright, was a mining engineer responsible for the coal mines of the Butterley Company. Five generations of the family had been involved in this Derbyshire company since it's foundation in 1790. David went to High School at Ampleforth College whence he won a minor scholarship in Classics to Pembroke College, Oxford. Deciding to spend two years doing his National Service before going to Oxford, he joined the Sherwood Foresters, was commissioned and spent a year in Malaya as a platoon commander, partly in the jungle, partly at the base camps. In 1969, on emerging from the army, he joined the Benedictine Community at Ampleforth Abbey in Yorkshire taking the name Ralph (pronounced Rafe) after the Derbyshire martyr, Ralph Sherwin.

Having completed his BA in Greats (Classics, Ancient History & Philosophy) at Oxford and his STL in Theology at Fribourg (Switzerland) he was ordained priest at Ampleforth Abbey on July 5, 1970. A month later, he left England, at the Abbot's invitation, to join the St. Louis Priory – the community's foundation in the United States. When the monastery became independent in July, 1973, he opted to become a permanent member of the newly independent house. Shortly thereafter, he became an American citizen. Fr. Ralph initially taught Latin, Greek, English and Religion in the St. Louis Priory School. In 1978, he was made Novice Master. He has been the Varsity Tennis coach on and off for over 25 years and Vocation Director for the community for about 20. Currently, besides running the Varsity tennis program and coordinating community efforts to attract vocations, he teaches Theology to the 11th grade, Creative Writing to seniors, and is Advisor in the School.

OTHER BOOKS BY FR. RALPH WRIGHT

Wild...
They Also Serve: Tennis, a Global Religion
Leaves of Water
On Leaves and Flowers and Trees
Life is Simpler Toward Evening
Ripples of Stillness
All the Stars are Snowflakes
Perhaps God
Christ Our Love for All Seasons
Our Daily Bread
The Eloquence of Truth
Mostly Vertical Thoughts

Over 50 Hymns

CPSIA information can be obtained at www.ICGtesting.com
Printed in the USA
LVOW092316200412

278469LV00003B/5/P